AUTHOR'S NOTE

In visiting Israel, and spending time with residents of a variety of backgrounds, races, and religions, it has struck me as very beautiful that so many people have such a powerful connection with Israel as their country. These intense feelings can sometimes lead to problems, but I find it extraordinary that Israel has this strong grip on us, so that we each think of it as "my Israel."

For the wonderful people at PJ Library, who provided the inspiration for this book.
—Alice Blumenthal McGinty

To my beloved family.
—Rotem Teplow

MY ISRAEL AND ME

Alice Blumenthal McGinty

ILLUSTRATED BY Rotem Teplow

Kalaniot Books
Moosic, Pennsylvania

By the hob-knobby trunk
of the baobab tree,
near the salt-crusted shores
of the misty Dead Sea,

I live in the place
where I most love to be...
here in my country,
my Israel and me.

The country of Israel is small—as small as the state of New Jersey. But within this tiny place are snow-capped mountains, deserts, hills, and seas. The people of Israel are as varied as its landscape. They come from many different backgrounds and live in cities, villages, farms, and more. Come meet the people of Israel!

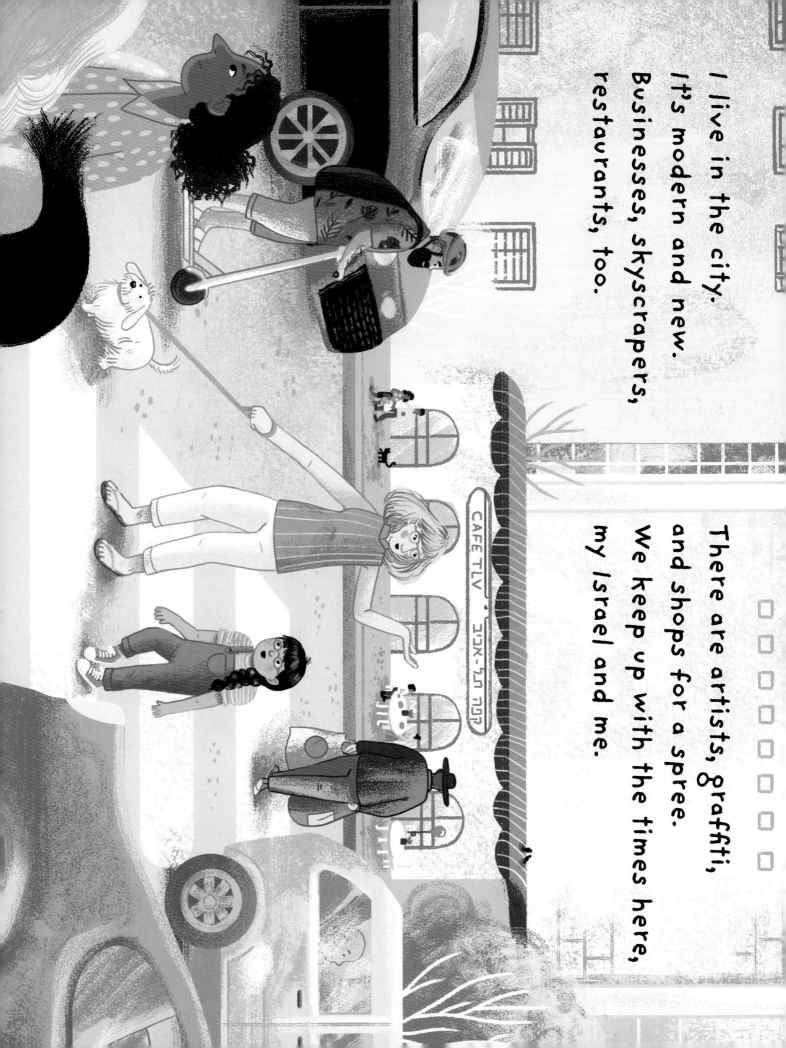

I live in the city.
It's modern and new.
Businesses, skyscrapers,
restaurants, too.

There are artists, graffiti,
and shops for a spree.
We keep up with the times here,
my Israel and me.

CAFE TLV
קפה תל-אביב

The biggest cities in Israel are Jerusalem and Tel Aviv. While Jerusalem is historic, Tel Aviv is very modern. Built on the shores of the Mediterranean Sea, Tel Aviv is a major business center. It has skyscrapers, shopping malls, and museums. The artists in Israel's cities are active as well, making jewelry, paintings, sculptures, and more.

On the kibbutz where I live
near a long, rolling hill,
we grow oranges, lemons,
olives, and dill.

I nibble persimmons
straight from the tree.
We are sun-kissed and growing,
my Israel and me.

Israel has a warm, sunny climate, and many people work the land, planting and tending to orchards and farms which grow many kinds of fruits, vegetables, and herbs. Some people in Israel live on a kibbutz, which is a community where the work is shared. Many kibbutzim have farms. Others run businesses such as hotels, or make products such as furniture.

We started a company
just last July.
I had an idea
and we gave it a try.

With our hip high-tech products
and bright employees,
we're shaping the future,
my Israel and me.

7

Israel has been called the "Start-up Nation," because it is home to over 6,000 start-up businesses. Many of these are high-tech companies, developing innovations such as instant messaging systems, medical technologies, cell phones, speedy battery chargers, and more. Even though it is a country of only about 9 million people, Israel is a world leader in technology.

I wander down alleys
and thin, winding streets.
The shopkeepers pet me,
and feed me my treats.

There are a lot of stray cats in Israel, which can be seen wandering the streets and alleys of Jerusalem and other cities. It is said that cats were brought into the country many years ago by the British to help get rid of rats. Now, the people and shop owners of the cities help take care of the cats by putting out bowls of food and water for them.

I'm a Jerusalem cat.
Look down and you'll see.
I'm glad you've discovered
my Israel and me.

I traveled to Israel
from lands far away.
I came here to live,
to study, and pray.

We can be as we want now.

My family is free.

We've made a new home here,

my Israel and me.

Many refugees come to Israel to escape a difficult life in other countries and return to the land of their ancestors. In Israel, they are free to make a living and practice their religion. Along with refugees, Israel has welcomed immigrants from places around the world, including Russia, America, France, and many countries in Africa. This makes Israel a diverse country, with residents—and foods—from all over the world.

In this small, simple home
near our goats and our sheep,
the land and our animals
earn us our keep.

We, the Bedouin people,
make meat, cheese, and tea.
We're one with the land here,
my Israel and me.

The name "Bedouin" means "desert people." These tribes of Arabs have lived in the Middle East for thousands of years as wandering, nomadic shepherds. Though most Bedouin in Israel now live in cities or villages, they still lead a simple life, raising sheep and goats and selling the products they make, such as goat's milk cheese, butter, and meat. They're also known for welcoming visitors with a fragrant cup of Bedouin tea.

I buy challah each Friday,
go to market for fish,
make a big Sabbath meal,
and share every dish.

On Shabbat, many stores close.
We're with family.
It's a true Sabbath rest
for my Israel and me.

Families observe the Sabbath in many different ways. In cities such as Jerusalem where stores and markets close for Shabbat from Friday evening to Saturday evening, observant Jews shop and prepare for the Sabbath on Friday afternoon. That evening, they eat a big Sabbath dinner, often inviting visitors, and attend services as the sun sets. During Shabbat, they don't work, cook, or drive. The Sabbath is spent in study and prayer, with family.

I'm an Arab Israeli.
Five times a day,
a call from the mosque nearby
bids me to pray.

Five times each day, in villages or cities such as Jerusalem and Haifa where many Arabs live, the slow, soulful Muslim call to prayer rings out from the mosques to signal time for praying. About 20% of Israel's population is Arab, and around 80% of them are Muslim. Many Arab families lived in Israel before the state was formed in 1948. Now, most speak both Arabic and Hebrew, and live as Israeli citizens.

I'm also a student and I'll earn my degree.

Yes, we're learning and prayerful, my Israel and me.

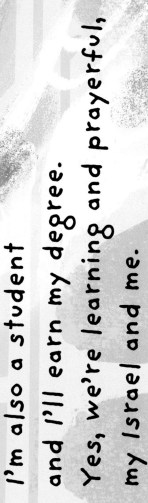

I visit this country.
I walk through the sand.
The biblical stories
took place on this land!

And though I don't live here,
my friends all agree...
it feels like our homeland,
my Israel and me.

Many people visit Israel every year, from countries all over the world. Tourists often travel to Israel to feel close to their religious history and homeland. In Jerusalem, for example, Jews may pray at the Western Wall, Christians may walk up the Mount of Olives, and Muslims may visit the Dome of the Rock.

In the midst of the desert,
we've turned brown to green.
We've constructed a reservoir,
filled a ravine.

When you see all the trees here,
you won't disagree.
We've brought life to the desert,
my Israel and me.

The Negev Desert covers over 60% of Israel, and Israelis have worked to grow trees, plants, and crops in the dry, sandy soil. They lead the world in new technologies to water crops, such as drip irrigation, which slowly releases water through tubes. They've also built reservoirs, learned to clean and recycle dirty water, and conserve rainwater that floods desert ravines.

We live here together,
each our own way.
In orchards, in cities,
we eat, work, and play.

This is our Israel.
We all play a part.
From people to people,
our home and our heart.